SPIRITUAL POEMS

FROM AN UNSCHOOLED SPIRIT

SPIRITUAL POEMS

FROM AN UNSCHOOLED SPIRIT

BY

LANCE CRAWFORD

Dick,
Prayers for you
and yours,
Lance

Bookstand Publishing

www.bookstandpublishing.com

Published by
Bookstand Publishing
Morgan Hill, CA 95037
3346_5

ISBN 978-1-58909-926-5

Printed in the United States of America

This book is dedicated in Memory of
My mother
E. Jane Crawford
She gave me life and a life model to emulate.

Also
Special thanks to my wife, Sandy, and her prayer group
for their support and prayers.

To the Tuesday Bible Study Class at St. Mark's Church
for opening so many doors.

To Felix Eddy for the wonderful cover design.

A Living Bible

A living Bible, that is what we are supposed to be.
Christ has given that commission to you and me.

We need not be all the pages found cover to cover,
It may be our role adds up to be something other.

Called to live a Christian life and spread the word,
The first of Christ some others have seen or heard.

Do this with our lives and others may take heed,
And you may be the first Bible that they ever read.

Moments in Time

OUR LIVES MAY TAKE YEARS FOR US TO LIVE,
     BUT IN TRUTH ARE JUST *MOMENTS IN TIME.*

WE STRUGGLE WITH THE MEANING TO THEM WE'LL GIVE,
     WHEN LIVING OUR PRECIOUS FEW *MOMENTS IN TIME.*

OTHER LIVES WITH OURS HAVE BECOME INTERLACED,
     AND WE EXIST IN EACH OTHER'S *MOMENTS IN TIME.*

WHAT MEASURE WAS USED WHEN VALUES WERE PLACED?
     WHEN LOOKING BACK ON THOSE *MOMENTS IN TIME.*

WHEN A LIFE IS LIVED WITH NO REASON OR RHYME
     IT HAS WASTED AWAY ITS OWN *MOMENTS IN TIME.*

A LIFE LIVED IN FULL VERSE TRANSCENDS THE MIME,
     AND HONORS AND GLORIFIES ITS *MOMENTS IN TIME.*

WE LIVE, WE LOVE, WE HAVE FAITH, AND WE BELIEVE,
     THAT A LIFE CAN ECLIPSE ITS *MOMENTS IN TIME.*

THROUGH FAITH IN HIM AND BY HIS GRACE WE WILL RECEIVE
     FROM GOD - *MOMENTS DIVINE.*

Hope's Sweet Song

Amid the worry, pain, and fears of a time when life is so nearly done,
We seek peace and comfort in prayer as hope's sweet song is sung.

It's through our own hope and the hopes of all those held dear,
That God's very presence in our life will comfort and allay all fear.

Embrace now the joy of life and celebrate all blessings we receive,
For there's nothing bad in the future of those who truly believe.

Memories are things to cherish, held both by us and those we love,
As a future not yet revealed is being written by a divine hand above.

Life's story is a true mystery with numbered chapters that unfold,
A life long journey that runs through time until the story is told.

Then hope's sweet song will have found God's heavenly ear,
His hand reaching out to touch us and wipe away our every tear.

For when it comes the time when all flesh must give up its mortal fight,
We put fears away seeing the glory of a spirit starting its eternal flight.

We should never doubt that it's to Heaven where they are ascending,
For in God it's not just a hope, but a promise of life that has no ending.

THE DEW

God has wonderfully created us and granted us a place
In the world that is also the work of His holy hands.

When God finished the world a smile graced his face,
He was so well pleased with the creation of the lands.

Then he created other creatures both large and small.
Man and woman came next and were especially blessed.

Give thought to the role that water has played in it all,
From the womb to the time baptism vows are professed.

God uses water when upon us the Holy Spirit he bestows.
Water serves as a symbol of God's pleasure here on earth.

He sends rain that sustains life in everything that grows,
And each dawn he cloaks it with dew to affirm its worth.

When a new child is baptized our baptism vows we renew.
God does the same for the earth with each drop of dew.

God truly loves all of His creation, that is plain to see.
The stewardship of it he has entrusted to you and me.

5

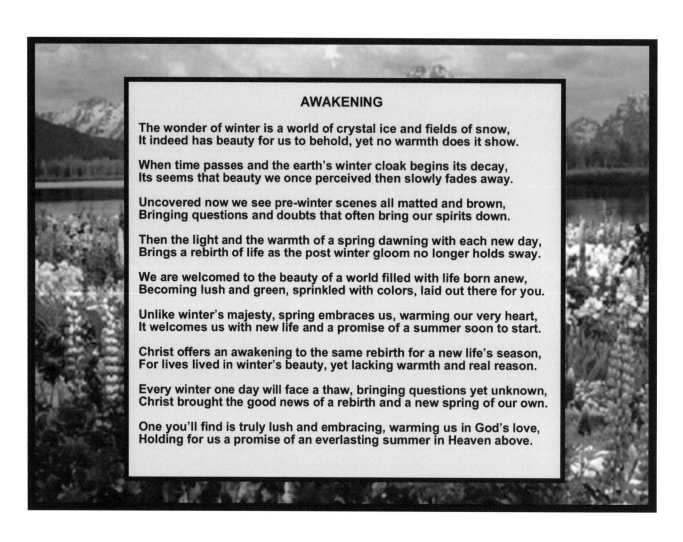

AWAKENING

The wonder of winter is a world of crystal ice and fields of snow,
It indeed has beauty for us to behold, yet no warmth does it show.

When time passes and the earth's winter cloak begins its decay,
Its seems that beauty we once perceived then slowly fades away.

Uncovered now we see pre-winter scenes all matted and brown,
Bringing questions and doubts that often bring our spirits down.

Then the light and the warmth of a spring dawning with each new day,
Brings a rebirth of life as the post winter gloom no longer holds sway.

We are welcomed to the beauty of a world filled with life born anew,
Becoming lush and green, sprinkled with colors, laid out there for you.

Unlike winter's majesty, spring embraces us, warming our very heart,
It welcomes us with new life and a promise of a summer soon to start.

Christ offers an awakening to the same rebirth for a new life's season,
For lives lived in winter's beauty, yet lacking warmth and real reason.

Every winter one day will face a thaw, bringing questions yet unknown,
Christ brought the good news of a rebirth and a new spring of our own.

One you'll find is truly lush and embracing, warming us in God's love,
Holding for us a promise of an everlasting summer in Heaven above.

Legacy

We live our lives on earth for only just a short stay,
Decisions and actions confronting us every day.

The kind of choices and actions we choose to make,
Determine the direction and path our lives will take.

We often fail to pause and reflect, so we may not see,
If the true value of our life is all that it was meant to be.

There will be good and bad in the things we've done.
Where will God figure in this our life's race we've run?

What measure will others use for the path we chose?
It will be written in the book that at the end we close.

When a life is over and one's work on earth is done,
What determines whether the battle is lost or won?

What we've done for us dies at death bell's chime,
What we've done for others lives on throughout time.

As Eagles Fly

Majestic eagles are the most powerful of birds,
So often portrayed in pictures, deeds, and words.

They show great strength in the beat of powerful wings,
In sharp talons they can carry heavy fish or other things,

On short runs they fly by strength to get somewhere,
As forceful wing strokes propel them through the air.

However, when hours are spent soaring in the sky,
We cannot help marveling and wondering why

Those powerful wings need not be moved at all.
And yet they glide effortlessly with no hint of a fall.

God's breath on the earth is warmed by the sun on high,
And eagles ride the thermals and all day cruise the sky.

Now consider how this all might relate to you and me.
God equips us with powerful bodies and minds you see,

And we use the strength of them to get us somewhere.
In the short run this determines how well we fare.

But if we are to also soar and be borne higher aloft,
God also gives us a thermal to ride in a breath so soft.

Faith that carries us above life's stresses and strife,
Born of the Holy Spirit God breathes into our life.

Then others seeing us will wonder and marvel why,
Our lives soar as our spirits rise so effortlessly high.

Random Acts

Things take place and they can have a great deal of effect on our life,
There are things that bring great joy, or things that can cause great strife.

Things that happen without apparent reason always give us pause,
As creatures of reason, we always want to know what was the cause.

If we look to thank the divine when there are random acts for the good,
Can we not also place the blame for bad there, as many think we should?

It's a mystery where the answer eludes the very bounds of our reason,
And for it man has proposed almost every explanation he can seize on.

So in the case when things occur randomly and lead to such tragic ends,
Be they by some human hand or by the rampant power that nature sends.

Their very randomness makes it hard to ascribe them to some Godly plan,
Ascribe them rather to nature's normal workings or the freewill acts of man.

Then what of random acts of kindness that so affect us, and our lives enrich,
Can we then completely remove God from this equation even if it's our wish?

Even though they may not be accomplished by God's holy hand on its own,
Such acts may grow out of knowing one whose example to us is well known.

In following Christ the doors are open to a wondrous life full of selfless acts,
Evolving from and carried out based on a faith, rather than simply on facts.

So even if those acts are not the sole providence of a hand from up above,
They remain a testament to the example of Christ and the power of his love.

Weathering a Storm

In troubled times when storms round us may rage,
Many of us often do only things we think are sage.

We look for a refuge in any place safe and warm,
Then try using our best efforts to avoid the storm.

But there will be times we are called to take action,
Then the courage of our hearts must find traction.

Where do we find the courage to take our stand,
As we face the storm and take troubles in hand?

It's in knowing that no matter the troubles we face,
God is with us with His strength and saving grace.

Realizing what a strength we have in our Lord,
We're amazed to find a courage in us restored.

Newly empowered now for action we must take,
And having God to guide the decisions we make.

Trouble's storm may continue against us to rage,
With God beside us our courage comes of age.

And although we find at times first efforts may fail,
With courage, faith, and persistence we will prevail.

Let this be a witness to God and others be shown,
With God our troubles are never ours to face alone.

A Firm Faith

Some who can quote scripture chapter and verse,
When misfortune comes lose faith and the Lord do curse.

Saying woe is me, becoming resentful and so very mad,
Blaming God for letting things happen that are so bad,
Never considering that as bad as things are, they could be worse.

Others are those who in those same troubled days,
Will keep their faith and the Lord still do praise.

Knowing that it wasn't God who caused the wrong,
They can rely on the Lord to keep them strong.
A solid faith can comfort the hurting in powerful ways.

A good time faith, like piled up sand, storms soon wash away.
While a rock solid faith can weather storms forever and a day.

A faith that is tested and yet remains unbroken,
Is a prayer that is heard, even though unspoken.
Being firm in your faith puts God in your life to stay.

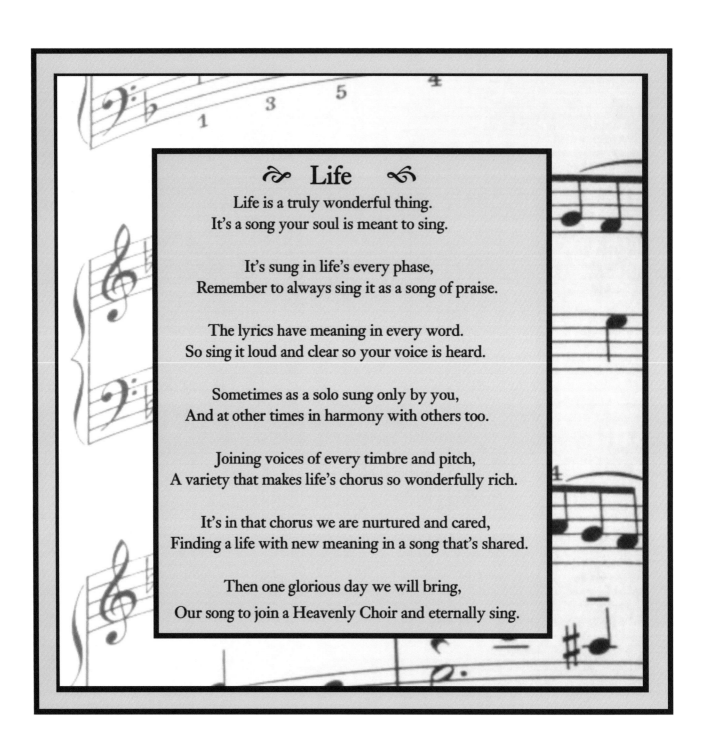

℘ Life ℘

Life is a truly wonderful thing.
It's a song your soul is meant to sing.

It's sung in life's every phase,
Remember to always sing it as a song of praise.

The lyrics have meaning in every word.
So sing it loud and clear so your voice is heard.

Sometimes as a solo sung only by you,
And at other times in harmony with others too.

Joining voices of every timbre and pitch,
A variety that makes life's chorus so wonderfully rich.

It's in that chorus we are nurtured and cared,
Finding a life with new meaning in a song that's shared.

Then one glorious day we will bring,
Our song to join a Heavenly Choir and eternally sing.

What About Others?

Life is like a road along which all of us must travel on the journey we take.
We travel not alone and the acquaintances of many fellow travelers we make.

Then what are we called to give others while we take our walk along life's way?
We will give it to others in how we act, by the things we do, and what we say.

Others can be seen to be likenesses of ourselves in existing in another being.
So as we find honor in ourselves, it's honor for themselves they'll be seeing.

We find the secret that's not so secret is Christ's message of the power of love.
The love we show to others, when mirroring the love God showers from above.

When we can give to others ourselves, ones that are honest, sweet, and pure.
It's a gift that when freely given, becomes an act of Godly love to long endure.

Abide then in God's grace and by that grace continue in His image to reside.
Sharing the way with others, loving them as yourself, and walking side by side.

Daybreak

Throughout the night darkness has held the dawn at bay,
Then dawn awakens and slowly pushes darkness away.

In dawn's soft light wondrous views can now be seen,
Nature is revealed in the lushness of its cloaks of green,

The light has silenced the sound of the owl's mournful cry.
Now the morning birds are lifting their songs toward the sky.

The pleasure is just to be there and breathe new sweet air,
As our eyes drink in the beauty and wonder of nature's fare.

But the break of day has just started, it's by no means done,
We await the crowning glory in the appearance of the sun.

And what an appearance it makes to the start of a new day,
It starts not with a burst of glory, but just with a single ray.

Filtering its way through nature's maze of branch and leaf.
Seeking a spot where it will create joy from a night of grief.

The sight, when it has found a perfect place, must be seen,
As things once only green, now glow with a golden sheen.

Then suddenly this is echoed with the coming of ray after ray,
As the sun's appearance works to complete the break of day.

There are people, who have yet to see the full light of day,
Never standing so the light of God's son will come their way.

When they do, they too will take on that same wonderful glow.
Touched by that light a new relationship with Christ will grow.

Those that are the first to be bathed in the glow of God's light,
Then reflect it on others making a new day wonderfully bright.

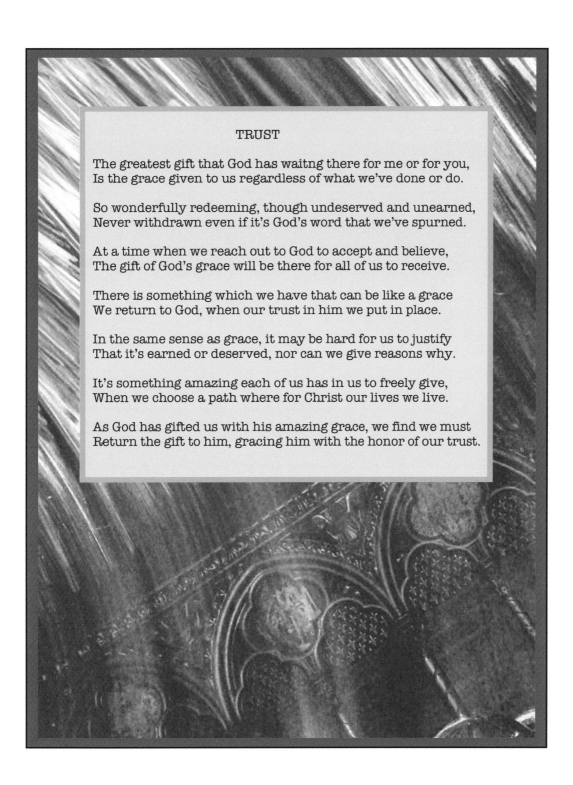

TRUST

The greatest gift that God has waitng there for me or for you,
Is the grace given to us regardless of what we've done or do.

So wonderfully redeeming, though undeserved and unearned,
Never withdrawn even if it's God's word that we've spurned.

At a time when we reach out to God to accept and believe,
The gift of God's grace will be there for all of us to receive.

There is something which we have that can be like a grace
We return to God, when our trust in him we put in place.

In the same sense as grace, it may be hard for us to justify
That it's earned or deserved, nor can we give reasons why.

It's something amazing each of us has in us to freely give,
When we choose a path where for Christ our lives we live.

As God has gifted us with his amazing grace, we find we must
Return the gift to him, gracing him with the honor of our trust.

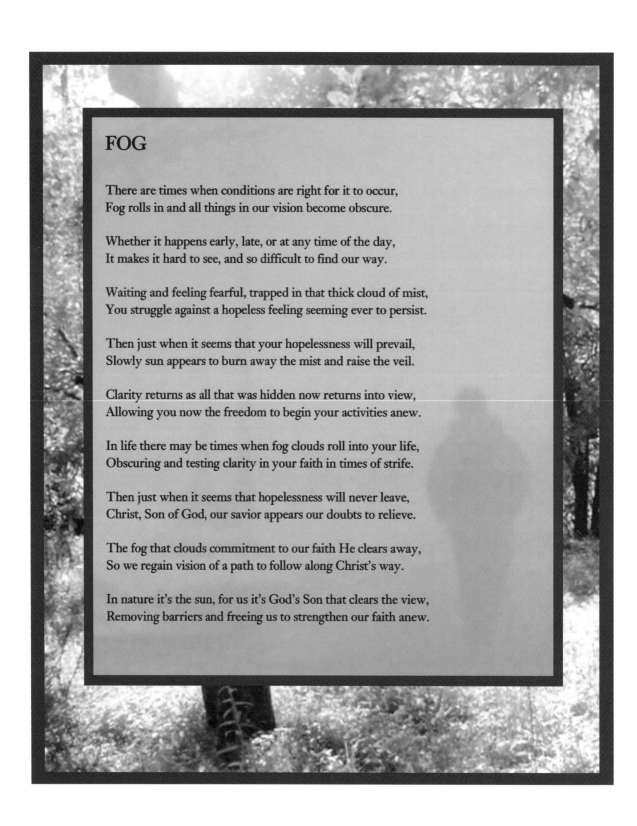

FOG

There are times when conditions are right for it to occur,
Fog rolls in and all things in our vision become obscure.

Whether it happens early, late, or at any time of the day,
It makes it hard to see, and so difficult to find our way.

Waiting and feeling fearful, trapped in that thick cloud of mist,
You struggle against a hopeless feeling seeming ever to persist.

Then just when it seems that your hopelessness will prevail,
Slowly sun appears to burn away the mist and raise the veil.

Clarity returns as all that was hidden now returns into view,
Allowing you now the freedom to begin your activities anew.

In life there may be times when fog clouds roll into your life,
Obscuring and testing clarity in your faith in times of strife.

Then just when it seems that hopelessness will never leave,
Christ, Son of God, our savior appears our doubts to relieve.

The fog that clouds commitment to our faith He clears away,
So we regain vision of a path to follow along Christ's way.

In nature it's the sun, for us it's God's Son that clears the view,
Removing barriers and freeing us to strengthen our faith anew.

ON BENDED KNEE

Addressing God we do want him to know,
How honor and respect to Him we show.

So in order that we may more humble be,
We often pray to Him on a bended knee.

Another reason just came to me one day,
For us to be on our knees when we pray.

It's a posture putting shoulders right in place,
Ready for God's hands to apply their grace.

Then His hands will lift our troubles away,
Replacing them with love in His caring way.

What a loving Lord that we call on in prayer,
Knowing when we're troubled he'll be there.

So when you pray, now pray on bended knee,
Waiting for Christ to lift your troubles free.

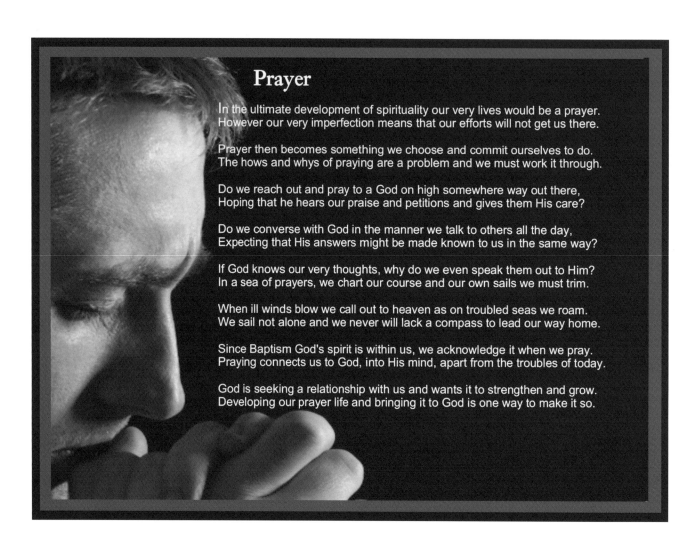

Prayer

In the ultimate development of spirituality our very lives would be a prayer.
However our very imperfection means that our efforts will not get us there.

Prayer then becomes something we choose and commit ourselves to do.
The hows and whys of praying are a problem and we must work it through.

Do we reach out and pray to a God on high somewhere way out there,
Hoping that he hears our praise and petitions and gives them His care?

Do we converse with God in the manner we talk to others all the day,
Expecting that His answers might be made known to us in the same way?

If God knows our very thoughts, why do we even speak them out to Him?
In a sea of prayers, we chart our course and our own sails we must trim.

When ill winds blow we call out to heaven as on troubled seas we roam.
We sail not alone and we never will lack a compass to lead our way home.

Since Baptism God's spirit is within us, we acknowledge it when we pray.
Praying connects us to God, into His mind, apart from the troubles of today.

God is seeking a relationship with us and wants it to strengthen and grow.
Developing our prayer life and bringing it to God is one way to make it so.

Loving a Stranger

I've been called to love a stranger, someone I don't even know,
And been told doing so is vital for my own spiritual life to grow.

The temptation is to think it's an opportunity for me to try to teach,
Or then drawing upon my personal religious beliefs begin to preach.

It's not a place or time for that, instead it's a time to practice openness,
Not overreact, but to listen and be open to the cause of their distress.

The ability to demonstrate love will come when I can see the he in me,
And then love's acceptance by him will come if he can see the me in he.

Then through caring and sharing, openness becomes a two-way street,
Where demonstrating love to a stranger becomes a less daunting feat.

May I then grow often more open, not turning away to avoid the strife,
And more closely follow the teachings and example of Christ in my life.

Silence

Be silent now and take the time,
To quiet our lips and play the mime.

Spiritual things expanding their bounds,
As we forsake the din of worldly sounds.

Giving honor to a God ever endearing,
In silence we now find a new hearing.

Attending to God in silence we truly hear,
How God speaks silently, and yet so clear.

We awaken to what we have heard,
As God quietly reveals to us His word.

Imagine the meaning we might have missed,
If life's distractions had not been dismissed.

Surely then our soul will find its own voice,
Raising it to sing God's praises and rejoice.

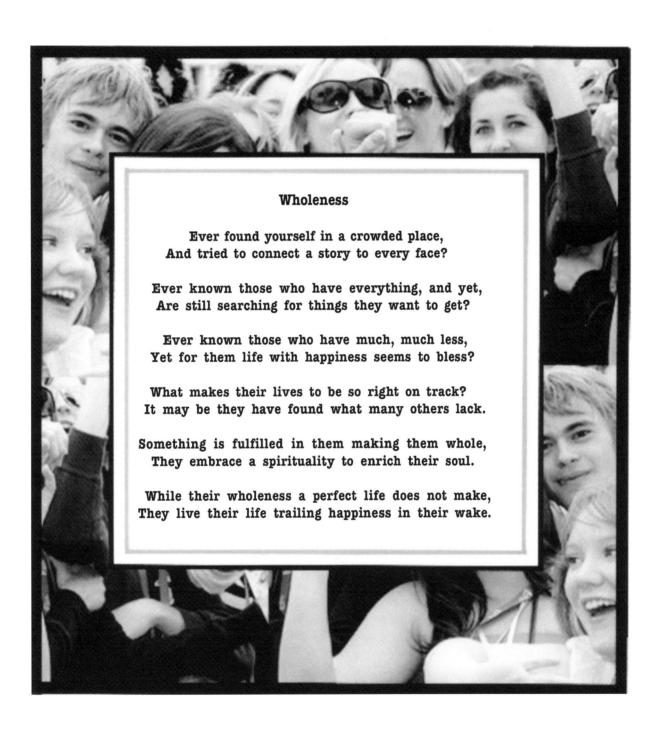

Wholeness

Ever found yourself in a crowded place,
And tried to connect a story to every face?

Ever known those who have everything, and yet,
Are still searching for things they want to get?

Ever known those who have much, much less,
Yet for them life with happiness seems to bless?

What makes their lives to be so right on track?
It may be they have found what many others lack.

Something is fulfilled in them making them whole,
They embrace a spirituality to enrich their soul.

While their wholeness a perfect life does not make,
They live their life trailing happiness in their wake.

POTTERY

Jesus was trained as a carpenter learning from Joseph that worthy trade,
But Christ is remembered more for what he taught than what he made.

God is the maker of everything and is still creating to this very day.
We are his creation as we are born of this earth and molded like clay.

Taken as clay from the dry soil and moistened in baptism it gives us form.
Then from that shapeless mass and in God's hands our life's future is born.

Before God decides exactly what he will create of us in his loving way,
He has to knead us with lessons and teachings to prepare the new clay.

God's hand's work firm and strong, wedging and getting our fiber in line.
Making clay that will take form on life's spinning wheel and hold up fine.

A little grit must be added so when worked, the clay's shape will hold firm.
Then clay unformed is now put on a wheel ready for God's hands to turn.

The clay is centered, being guided gently but firmly by God's loving hands,
And where there once was shapeless lump, a balanced cone now stands.

Then the forming begins as God's fingers draw the potential from the clay,
Creating each one of us different to serve God's purpose in our own way.

Now our design has been created and now wonderfully formed we stand,
Ready for firing in the heat of life's kiln and face whatever life will demand.

Pottery crafted and formed with a purpose and use ordained by the Lord,
We are pottery that when serving him is both our mission and our reward.

Daily

As Christians we are called to be in relationship with Christ every day,
In our humanity all too often we give into temptations that lead us astray.

In doing so we blanket over our souls and create an alternate kind of me,
One that in our minds would be what we think others would like to see.

This puts our relationship with Christ under a great deal of stress,
Changing our personalities, manners and even the way we may dress.

We may choose to wear the cloth and clothes that we see others wear.
We adopt a presence to show others without ourselves even being there.

If we have wealth we can buy the most regal and the finest looking things,
Often leaving us unaware and unprepared for the danger that this brings.

The value and importance we place on the material of fashions we own,
Changes us and we soon find that into a different person we've grown.

Rather we should start with just one thread from what clothed our Lord,
And weave a cloak that when worn will find our soul soon be restored.

Differences now disappear and we now truly are as we are seen to be,
Reestablishing the spiritual bond that between us Christ wants us to see.

And when we daily find ourselves doing any mindless or mundane thing,
Simply rub softly on that cloak until suddenly your soul begins to sing.

LIFE STORIES

Our knowledge about our lives develops as we have grown.
It's our own story and to us and those close to us well known.

There are relationships and memories we have by the score,
Just imagine all the facts and figures those memories store.

And yet all this about us is only a page in a much larger book.
We can find many stories of others when we take the time to look.

So when we get so deeply caught up only in the lives of our own,
Consider the chapters about others in a more compassionate tone.

Mindful that everyone whose path we cross in an average day,
Writes a page in life's book just as important as ours in every way.

When we get caught up only in ourselves, it's time we should start
Remembering the place Christians keep neighbors in their heart.

Pick up the book our lives are written in and open to other pages.
Reading there will unfold the lives of others in all their many stages.

Stories of others filled with needs, hopes and dreams of their own,
How will we measure up concerning the love to them we've shown?

May reviewers exclaim after our page they've had a chance to scan,
"That's a story reflecting the life of a Christian woman or man."

A person who sees interests and concerns beyond their own life's story,
Is someone who appreciates and celebrates the whole world to God's glory.

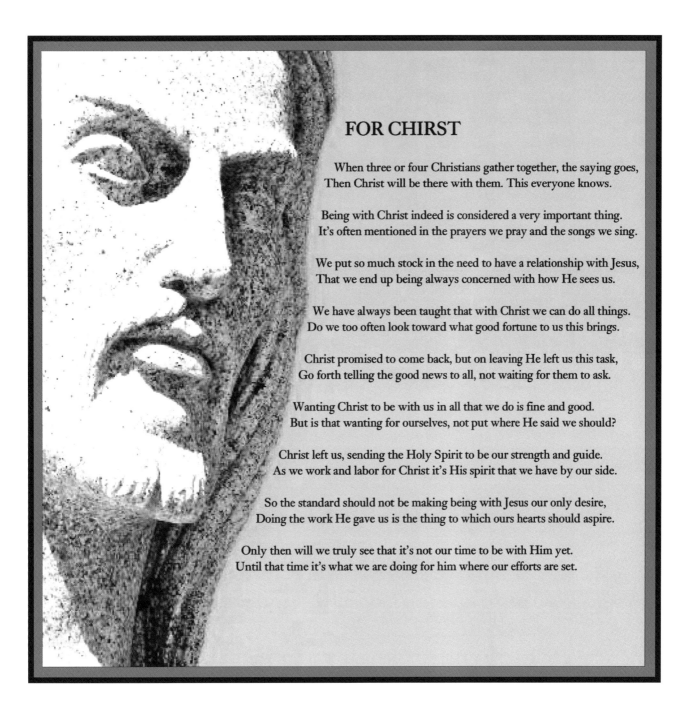

FOR CHIRST

When three or four Christians gather together, the saying goes,
Then Christ will be there with them. This everyone knows.

Being with Christ indeed is considered a very important thing.
It's often mentioned in the prayers we pray and the songs we sing.

We put so much stock in the need to have a relationship with Jesus,
That we end up being always concerned with how He sees us.

We have always been taught that with Christ we can do all things.
Do we too often look toward what good fortune to us this brings.

Christ promised to come back, but on leaving He left us this task,
Go forth telling the good news to all, not waiting for them to ask.

Wanting Christ to be with us in all that we do is fine and good.
But is that wanting for ourselves, not put where He said we should?

Christ left us, sending the Holy Spirit to be our strength and guide.
As we work and labor for Christ it's His spirit that we have by our side.

So the standard should not be making being with Jesus our only desire,
Doing the work He gave us is the thing to which ours hearts should aspire.

Only then will we truly see that it's not our time to be with Him yet.
Until that time it's what we are doing for him where our efforts are set.

EVERLASTING

A heart beats no more and now one earthly life is through.
It's something all must face when fate claims what's due.

We mourn and also rejoice, for our loss is heaven's gain,
And our loved one is now free from their suffering and pain.

Honor and give praise to Christ and the gift of love he gave,
For now our lives no longer end, they transcend the grave.

We give thanks for their lives and for what we have shared.
The memories we hold are a sign of how much they cared.

Love is a bond even the separation of death cannot break,
Like a passing ship that has left lasting ripples in its wake.

Spreading over the surface of life's waters, never ending,
Washing upon the shores where love ones stand tending.

With their nets in hand and on those waters always casting,
Constantly netting memories which make love everlasting.

26

ME

No matter how you and I our own holiness do foresee,
God is something that we should never pretend to be.

However, here's something we aren't trained to see,
It's that there exists a trinity in each of you and in me.

The first of the these three is how ourselves we see.
This may be wonderful or often less to some degree.

Next is what others see after spending time with me.
Can we really imagine what their true thoughts will be?

Third surely ranks the most important of all the three,
It is the me we hear God calling each one of us to be.

All three are one and the same person by our name.
Accomplish the third, all three will appear the same.

Ourselves and others will then rate us the same way,
As we live lives serving the Lord each and every day.

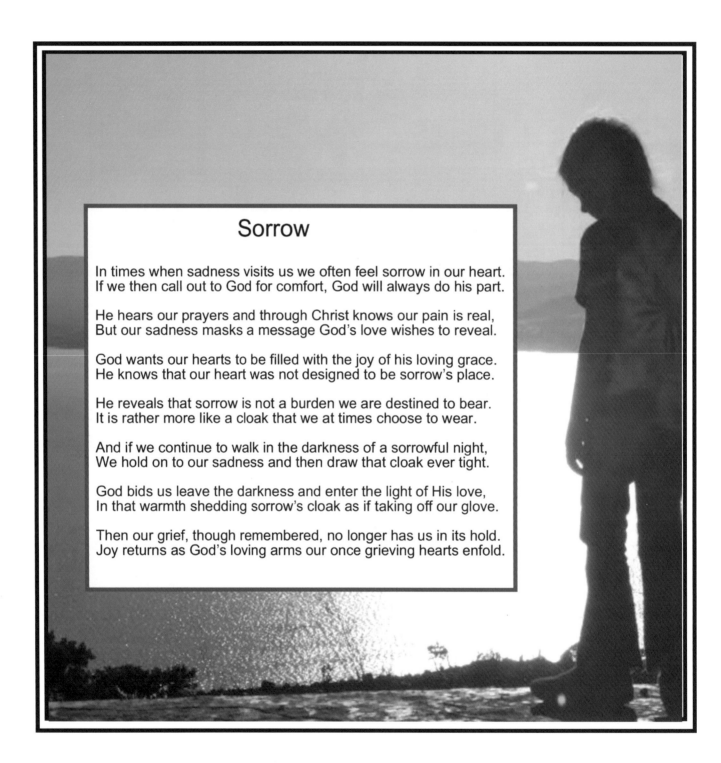

Sorrow

In times when sadness visits us we often feel sorrow in our heart.
If we then call out to God for comfort, God will always do his part.

He hears our prayers and through Christ knows our pain is real,
But our sadness masks a message God's love wishes to reveal.

God wants our hearts to be filled with the joy of his loving grace.
He knows that our heart was not designed to be sorrow's place.

He reveals that sorrow is not a burden we are destined to bear.
It is rather more like a cloak that we at times choose to wear.

And if we continue to walk in the darkness of a sorrowful night,
We hold on to our sadness and then draw that cloak ever tight.

God bids us leave the darkness and enter the light of His love,
In that warmth shedding sorrow's cloak as if taking off our glove.

Then our grief, though remembered, no longer has us in its hold.
Joy returns as God's loving arms our once grieving hearts enfold.

COMMUNITY

You may think that something we do out of choice or circumstance sets us apart,
Yet you'll find treating others with compassion is where community has its start.

Acknowledging we all never measure up to perfection on any personal scale,
But through compassion, imperfection is by no means a recipe for us to fail.

In community we find the spiritual development and strength for all that we face.
If common humanness connects us, it also opens us up to God and His grace.

We don't fail God because we fall short in our effort to make perfection our goal.
Failure is if we don't adopt compassion to make our spiritual lives more whole.

God is for us, about us, and in us. His knowing us leaves us with nothing to hide.
So mirror Christ in dealing with others, embracing God, and in His love abide.

Waves Evermore

When I walk along the ocean's shore,
I see the waves breaking evermore.

Like lemmings marching many strong,
Singing their steady and rhythmic song.

To the shore, their final leap making,
It seems it's their life they're forsaking.

But in truth of fact this is just not so,
As they recede unseen to then regrow.

So water, earth's lifeblood will ever live,
And to the earth an eternal pulse does give.

At rest and calm a pulse steady and slow,
Then storm excited its pace will quickly grow.

It reflects the earth having an active life,
With peaceful times and then times of strife.

There is a parallel for the life of our own,
In the calms and storms we've all known.

So when we all walk our life's own shore,
Find peace in the waves breaking evermore.

Humility

We arise each morn and start living the beginning of another new day.
We tackle chores, go off to work, and if we're lucky have time to play.

Ever pondered about what you're doing with the gifts God has given you?
Wondering if you're really using them in a way you were supposed to do.

The good Lord grants greatness not for you to be greatly served you see.
The greater the gifts you receive, the greater servant you're called to be.

God's justice often can be hard to understand for those like you and me.
The mystery can be solved and the answer is found in acts of humility.

Don't get so caught up in yourself and the importance of your life's story.
Identify your gifts, putting them to work for not your own, but God's glory.

Then will you receive others kindly, recognizing in them common humanity,
And with humility grow into all that God in his grace has prepared you to be.

The Hug

As I approached, my friend stood waiting with arms open wide,
Those arms drawing me forward as if waters of a rising tide.

With my friend standing with the sun setting from behind,
Silhouetted against the sky, suddenly a symbol came to mind.

Standing there I saw a cross where my friend was standing.
A cross that hosted Christ's sacrifice, now love demanding.

The cross arms of that cross became the arms of my friend,
To enfold me in the embrace of a hug with a message to send.

Imparting the meaning and warmth of Christ's undying love,
The warmth of a hug filled with caring that flows from above.

So we will continue to share a hug with those we hold dear,
Remembering that such an embrace shows affection so clear.

A cross that once could be found standing upon Calvary's hill,
Becomes a symbol of an embrace welcoming us to God's will.

WHY LOVE

HATE DESTROYS,
LOVE RESTORES

HATE IS PERSISTENT,
LOVE ENDURES

HATE DRIVES APART,
LOVE BINDS

HATE HAS VICTORIES,
LOVE PREVAILS

HATE IS SPECIFIC,
LOVE IS UNIVERSAL

HATE WITHERS,
LOVE BLOSSOMS

HATE SOURS,
LOVE SWEETENS

HATE DEFILES,
LOVE GLORIFIES

HATE ENDS WITH DEATH
LOVE IS ENTERNAL

CHOOSE LOVE

SAILING AWAY

THIS DAY YOU SAIL AWAY.

YOU ARE SO LOVED AND OUR WISH IS THAT YOU COULD STAY,
BUT INSTEAD WE'RE HERE THIS DAY TO SEE YOU SAIL AWAY.

THE OCEAN HAS CALLED WITH THE SONG WE KNOW SO WELL,
ITS VOICE CARRIED ON THE RISE AND FALL OF EVERY SWELL.

IT'S AN ETERNAL SONG AND SOME DAY IT WILL CALL US TOO.
HOWEVER TODAY THE SEAS HAVE SUNG AND ARE CALLING YOU.

AND ON THIS DAY YOU SAIL AWAY.

MAY YOU FIND THE BREEZE AND THE RIGHT WAVES TO RIDE,
AND JOURNEY FAR AND BE CARRIED BY EVERY EBB AND TIDE.

AS THOSE LEFT HERE ADD THEIR TEARS TO THE OCEAN'S FLOW,
FINDING COMFORT IN THE BEAUTY OF THE DAY'S SUNSET GLOW.

MISSING YOU BUT KNOWING IT'S A JOURNEY WE ALL WILL TAKE.
WE WILL CHERISH MEMORIES LEFT BY THE RIPPLES IN YOUR WAKE.

HEAVEN'S CHARTED AS YOUR COURSE AND WE ADD THIS PRAYER,
GODSPEED AND MAY STEADY BREEZES CARRY YOU SAFELY THERE.

THIS DAY AS YOU SAIL AWAY.

WRITTEN FOR MY SISTER GAIL MAY 24., 2009

CPSIA information can be obtained at www.ICGtesting.com
Printed in the USA
BVIW12n2358180816
459511BV00002B/2